1 MONTH OF
FREE
READING

at

www.ForgottenBooks.com

By purchasing this book you are eligible for one month membership to ForgottenBooks.com, giving you unlimited access to our entire collection of over 1,000,000 titles via our web site and mobile apps.

To claim your free month visit: www.forgottenbooks.com/free911261

ISBN 978-0-265-92889-9
PIBN 10911261

Historic, archived docume

Do not assume content reflects c
ientific knowledge, policies, or pr

SEPTEMBER 15, 1923

WHOLESALE PRICE LIST

Portland
Wholesale Nursery
Company

PACKING HOUSE AND
OFFICES
971 SANDY BOULEVARD
PORTLAND, ORE.

ALBERT BROWNELL, President
A. H. STEINMETZ, Vice President
D. S. BROWNELL, Sec. and Treas.

SEPTEMBER 15, 1923

WHOLESALE PRICE LIST

Portland Wholesale Nursery Company

PACKING HOUSE AND
OFFICES
971 SANDY BOULEVARD
PORTLAND, ORE.

———

ALBERT BROWNELL, President
A. H. STEINMETZ, Vice President
D. S. BROWNELL, Sec. and Treas.

A small block of our Japan Pear Seedlings between two blocks of two year Apple.

To Our Patrons

THIS Price List will be followed by Surplus Lists at intervals during the season. If you do not receive these we would consider it a favor if you will send us your name and address for our mailing list, and they will be mailed to you as issued.

Prices in this list are intended for the TRADE only. If this list reaches anyone not entitled to it, we would appreciate being advised of the fact, so we may correct our mailing list.

The new standard of grading adopted at the last meeting of the Pacific Coast Association of Nurserymen is used in this list. Kindly make your orders accordingly.

We do not employ Agents and no Dealers are authorized to use our name.

CANCELLATION.

We are glad to accommodate our customers by reselling stock they may have ordered from us and find they cannot use if we can find a market for it, but it is manifestly unfair to insist on our cancelling an order if we can not resell it, and in self-defense are obliged to refuse to do so.

SUBSTITUTION.

If you wish us to substitute in case we are sold short of any variety ordered, please so state, as we do not substitute unless requested to do so.

SHIPPING SEASON.

Our packing season commences from October 1st to October 15th and continues until from April 1st to May 1st, varying with the season.

GUARANTEE OF GENUINENESS.

While we exercise the greatest care to have every tree or plant true to name, and are ready, on proper proof, to replace anything sent out by us that may prove untrue to label, free of charge or refund the money paid for it, it is understood and agreed, between the purchaser and ourselves, that we are not to be held liable for any greater sum than that paid us for said trees that may prove untrue.

LOCATION.

We are located at 971 Sandy Boulevard, opposite the Old People's Home. To reach our place take Rose City Park cars on Washington Street, between Fifth and Second Streets, and get off at East Thirty-second street. You are invited to call on us when in the city, and we would take pleasure in taking you out to see our growing nursery stock, several good blocks of which are near town.

Terms and Conditions of Sale

PRICE nerein quoted are for first-class stock of the grades named, but are subject to change without notice.

Five of a variety will be furnished at the Ten rate, Fifty at the Hundred rate and Five Hundred at the Thousand rate.

Orders should be made on a separate sheet, and not in the body of a letter, always giving plainly the postoffice, destination and route the goods are to be forwarded by.

Our terms are cash or satisfactory references before shipment; to established nurserymen who are known to us, or who give the necessary references, a credit of 60 days from date of invoice will be allowed, with a discount of 3% for cash with order, 2% in 10 days, and 1% in 30 days. A liberal deposit is expected to be made on orders for future delivery. All bills must be paid by June 1st or interest accrues from then or any prior date of maturity, at the rate of 8% per annum. This does not apply on supplies, which are a cash proposition and handled on a close margin, partly as an accommodation.

C. O. D. orders must be accompanied by a remittance to cover one-third of the cost of the order.

If shipment is made to a prepay station, a remittance sufficient to cover the freight charges must accompany the order.

All orders will be carefully packed, for which a moderate charge will be made to cover the cost of material and labor.

All shipments are at the risk of the purchaser after being delivered in good condition to the forwarders. Purchaser must be responsible for any loss or delay that may occur through the negligence of forwarders or horticultural inspectors. We will use every means possible to secure prompt delivery but are not liable for delays in transit, and our responsibility will cease upon delivery in good order to the carrier company, and the remedy for loss must lay between the purchaser and carrier company.

All claims for shortage or damage must be made within ten days of receipt of stock, or they will not be allowed. We book all orders with the understanding that same shall be void should injury befall the stock from Flood, Fire, Frost, Drought, or other causes beyond our control.

Kindly address all orders or correspondence to the
PORTLAND WHOLESALE NURSERY CO.
971 Sandy Boulevard

Portland   -   -   -   -   Oregon

FRUIT TREES

APPLES AND CRABS, TWO YEAR

Caliper	Height	Per 10	Per 100	Per 1000
11/16-in. and up 5	-ft. and up....$4.00		$30.00	$250.00
5/8 to 11/16-in. 4	-ft. and up.... 3.00		25.00	225.00
1/2 to 5/8-in. 3½-ft. and up.... 2.50			17.50	150.00

Arkansas Black	Baldwin	Banana
Ben Davis	Bismarck	Delaware Red
Delicious	Early Harvest	Fameuse
Gano	Gravenstein	Grimes Golden
Jonathan	King	King David
Maidens Blush	Mam. Blacktwig	McIntosh
Northern Spy	N. W. Greening	Oldenburg
Ortley	Peter	Red Astrachan
R. C. Pippin	Red June	R. I. Greening
Rome Beauty	Spitzenberg	Stayman Winesap
Talman Sweet	Tetofsky	Wagener
Waxen	Wealthy	W. W. Pearmain
Winesap	Wolf River	Yel. Bellflower
Yellow Newtown	Yel. Transparent	
Hyslop	Transcendent	Whitney
Yellow Siberian		

A portion of one of our one year Apple blocks still growing rapidly

APPLES AND CRABS, ONE YEAR

Caliper	Height	Per 10	Per 100	Per 1000
5/8-in. and up 4	-ft. and up....$3.00		$25.00	$225.00
1/2 to 5/8-in. 3½-ft. and up.... 2.75			22.50	200.00
3/8 to 1/2-in. 3	-ft. and up.... 2.50		17.50	150.00
1/4 to 3/8-in. 2	-ft. and up.... 1.75		12.50	100.00

Alexander	Arkansas Black	Baldwin
Banana	Ben Davis	Delicious
Early Harvest	Fameuse	Gano
Gravenstein	Grimes Golden	Jonathan
King	King David	Maidens Blush
*Mam. Blacktwig	McIntosh	Northern Spy
Oldenburg	Ortley	Red Astrachan
*R. C. Pippin	Red Gravenstein	Red June
Red Rome Beauty	R. I. Greening	Rome Beauty
Spitzenberg	Stayman	Sweet Bough
Talman Sweet	Wagener	Waxen
Wealthy	White Astrachan	W. W. Pearmain
*Winesap	Yel. Bellflower	Yellow Newtown
Yel. Transparent		
Hyslop	Red Siberian	Transcendent
Whitney	Yellow Siberian	

PEARS, TWO YEAR

Caliper	Per 10	Per 100	Per 1000
$\frac{11}{16}$-in. and up	$4.50	$40.00	$350.00
⅝ to $\frac{11}{16}$-in.	4.00	35.00	325.00

Bosc and Winter Nelis 5c additional per tree in each grade.

Anjou	Clapps Favorite	Comice
Crocker Bartlett	Early Harvest	Flemish Beauty
Garber	Howell	Kieffer
Koonce	P. Barry	Seckel
Vicar	Wilder	Winter Bartlett
Winter Nelis	Worden Seckel	

PEARS, ONE YEAR

Caliper	Height	Per 10	Per 100	Per 1000
⅝-in. and up	4 -ft. and up	$4.00	$35.00	$325.00
½ to ⅝-in.	3½-ft. and up	3.75	32.50	300.00
⅜ to ½-in.	3 -ft. and up	3.50	27.50	250.00
¼ to ⅜-in.	2 -ft and up	3.00	22.50	200.00

Bosc and Winter Nelis 5c additional per tree in each grade.

Anjou	Bartlett	Bosc
Clapps Favorite	Comice	Crocker Bartlett
Early Harvest	Flemish Beauty	Hardy
Keiffer	Koonce	P. Barry
Seckel	Wilder	Winter Bartlett
Winter Nelis	Worden Seckel	

One year Bartlett Pear

QUINCES, ONE YEAR

Caliper	Height	Per 10	Per 100
½-in and up	3½-ft. and up....	$5.00	$45.00
⅜ to ½-in.	3 -ft. and up	4.50	40.00
¼ to ⅜-in.	2 -ft. and up....	3.50	30.00

Orange   Pineapple   Van Dieman

SWEET CHERRIES, ONE YEAR

Caliper	Height	Per 10	Per 100	Per 1000
¾-in. and up	5 -ft. and up....	$7.00	$60.00	
⅝ to ¾-in.	4 -ft. and up....	6.00	50.00	$450.00
½ to ⅝-in.	3½-ft. and up....	5.00	45.00	400.00
⅜ to ½-in.	3 -ft. and up....	4.50	40.00	350.00
¼ to ⅜-in.	2 -ft. and up....	3.50	30.00	250.00

Bing   Blk Republican   Blk Tartarian
Lambert   Royal Ann (Napoléon)
Waterhouse, L. S.

Sample of one year Sweet Cherry

SOUR CHERRIES, TWO YEARS

Caliper	Height	Per 10	Per 100	Per 1000
11/16-in and up	....	$6.00	$50.00	
⅝ to 11/16-in.	....	5.00	45.00	$400.00

Early Richmond   May Duke

SOUR CHERRIES, ONE YEAR

Caliper	Height	Per 10	Per 100	Per 1000
⅝-in. and up	3½-ft. and up....	$6.00	$50.00	
½ to ⅝-in.	3 -ft. and up....	5.00	45.00	$400.00
⅜ to ½-in.	2½-ft. and up....	4.50	40.00	350.00
¼ to ⅜-in.	2 -ft. and up....	3.50	30.00	250.00

Early Richmond Late Duke   May Duke
Montmorency

PLUMS ON PEACH, ONE YEAR

Caliper	Height	Per 10	Per 100	Per 1000
¾-in. and up	6-ft. and up	$4.00	$35.00	$300.00
⅝ to ¾-in.	5-ft. and up	3.75	32.50	275.00
½ to ⅝-in.	4-ft. and up	3.50	30.00	250.00
⅜ to ½-in.	3-ft. and up	3.00	25.00	200.00
¼ to ⅜-in.	2-ft. and up	2.50	20.00	150.00

Beauty   Blue Damson   Peach
Santa Rosa   Satsuma   Wickson

PLUMS ON MYROBOLAN, ONE YEAR

Caliper	Height	Per 10	Per 100	Per 1000
¾ in. and up	6-ft. and up	$4.50	$40.00	$350.00
⅝ to ¾-in.	5-ft. and up	4.25	37.50	325.00
½ to ⅝-in.	4-ft. and up	4.00	35.00	300.00
⅜ to ½-in	3-ft. and up	3.50	30.00	250.00
¼ to ⅜-in.	2-ft. and up	3.00	25.00	200.00

Blue Damson   Green Gage   Shropshire Damson

PRUNES ON PEACH, ONE YEAR

Caliper	Height	Per 10	Per 100	Per 1000
¾-in. and up	6-ft. and up	$4.00	$35.00	$300.00
⅝ to ¾-in.	5-ft. and up	3.75	32.50	275.00
½ to ⅝-in.	4-ft. and up	3.50	30.00	250.00
⅜ to ½-in.	3-ft. and up	3.00	25.00	200.00
¼ to ⅜-in.	2-ft. and up	2.50	20.00	150.00

French   French Improved   Imperial
Italian

Improved French Prune

8

PRUNES ON MYROBOLAN, ONE YEAR

Caliper	Height	Per 10	Per 100	Per 1000
¾-in and up	6-ft. and up......$4.50		$40.00	$350.00
⅝ to ¾-in.	5-ft. and up...... 4.25		37.50	325.00
½ to ⅝-in.	4-ft. and up...... 4.00		35.00	300.00
⅜ to ½-in.	3-ft. and up...... 3.50		30.00	250.00
¼ to ⅜-in.	2-ft. and up...... 3.00		25.00	200.00
French	French Improved	Italian		
Sugar	Tragedy			

PEACHES, ONE YEAR

Caliper	Height	Per 10	Per 100	Per 1000
⅝-in. and up	4 -ft. and up....$4.00		$35.00	
½ to ⅝-in.	3½-ft. and up.... 3.50		30.00	$250.00
⅜ to ½-in.	3 -ft. and up.... 3.00		25.00	200.00
¼ to ⅜-in.	2 -ft. and up.... 2.50		20.00	150.00
Crawfords Early	Crawfords Late	Early Elberta		
Elberta	J. H. Hale	Lovell		
Muir	Orange Cling, S.	Phillips Cling		
Salway	Slappy	Triumph		
Tuscan Cling				

APRICOTS ON PEACH, ONE YEAR

Caliper	Height	Per 10	Per 100	Per 1000
⅝-in. and up	4 -ft. and up....$4.50		$40.00	$350.00
½ to ⅝-in.	3½-ft and up.... 4.00		35.00	300.00
⅜ to ½-in.	3 -ft. and up.... 3.50		30.00	250.00
¼ to ⅜-in.	2 -ft. and up.... 3.00		25.00	200.00
Blenheim	Moorpark	Royal		
Wen. Moorpark				

APRICOTS ON MYROBOLAN, ONE YEAR

Caliper	Height	Per 10	Per 100	Per 1000
⅝-in. and up	4 -ft. and up....$5.00		$45.00	$400.00
½ to ⅝-in.	3½-ft and up.... 4.50		40.00	350.00
⅜ to ½-in.	3 -ft. and up.... 4.00		35.00	300.00
¼ to ⅜-in.	2 -ft. and up.... 3.50		30.00	250.00
Blenheim	Royal			

NECTARINES, ONE YEAR

Caliper	Height	Per 10	Per 100
½-in. and up	3½-ft. and up....$6.00		$50.00
⅜ to ½-in.	3 -ft. and up.... 5.50		45.00
¼ to ⅜-in.	2 -ft. and up.... 4.50		35.00
Boston	New White	Stanwick	

GRAPES

AMERICAN VARIETIES

Grown here and ready for fall delivery

	Per 10	Per 100	Per 1000
Campbells Early, 2 yr, No. 1..$1.75		$15.00	
Campbells Early, 2 yr, No. 2.. 1.50		12.50	$100.00
Campbells Early, 1 yr, No. 1.. 1.50		12.50	100.00
Concord, 2 year, No. 1............ 1.25		10.00	80.00
Concord, 2 year, No. 2............ 1.00		8.00	60.00
Concord, 1 year, No. 1............ 1.00		8.00	60.00
Delaware, 1 year, No. 1.......... 1.50		12.50	
Eaton, 2 year, No. 1................ 1.75		15.00	
Eaton, 2 year, No. 2............ 1.50		12.50	
Eaton, 1 year, No. 1................ 1.50		12.50	
Moores Early, 2 year, No. 1.. 1.75		15.00	125.00
Moores Early 2 year, No. 2.. 1.50		12.50	100.00
Moores Early, 1 year, No. 1.. 1.50		12.50	100.00
Niagara, 2 year, No. 1............ 1.50		12.50	100.00
Niagara, 2 year, No. 2............ 1.25		10.00	80.00
Niagara, 1 year, No. 1............ 1.25		10.00	80.00
Worden, 2 year, No. 1............ 1.50		12.50	100.00
Worden, 2 year, No. 2............ 1.25		10.00	80.00
Worden, 1 year, No. 1............ 1.25		10.00	80.00

SMALL FRUITS

GOOSEBERRIES

	Per 10	Per 100	Per 1000
Oregon Champion, 1 yr, No. 1	$ .60	$ 5.00	$ 40.00
Oregon Champion, 1 yr, No. 2	.50	4.00	30.00

CURRANTS

	Per 10	Per 100	Per 1000
Cherry, 2 year, No. 1	$ .75	$6.00	$50.00
Cherry, 2 year, No. 2	.60	5.00	40.00
Cherry, 1 year, No. 1	.60	5.00	40.00
Cherry, 1 year, No. 2	.50	4.00	30.00
Fays, 2 year, No. 1	.75	6.00	50.00
Fays, 2 year, No. 2	.60	5.00	40.00
Fays, 1 year, No. 1	.60	5.00	40.00
Fays, 1 year, No. 2	.50	4.00	30.00
London Market, 2 yr, No. 1	.75	6.00	50.00
London Market, 2 yr, No. 2	.60	5.00	40.00
London Market, 1 yr. No. 1	.60	5.00	40.00
London Market, 1 yr, No. 2	.50	4.00	30.00
North Star, 2 year, No. 1	.75	6.00	50.00
North Star, 2 year, No. 2	.60	5.00	40.00
North Star, 1 year, No. 1	.60	5.00	40.00
North Star, 1 year, No. 2	.50	4.00	30.00
Perfection, 2 year, No. 1	1.00	7.00	60.00
Perfection, 2 year, No. 2	.75	6.00	50.00
Perfection, 1 year, No. 1	.75	6.00	50.00
Perfection, 1 year, No. 2	.60	5.00	40.00
Red Dutch, 2 year, No. 1	.75	6.00	
Red Dutch, 2 year, No. 2	.60	5.00	
Red Dutch, 1 year, No. 1	.60	5.00	
Red Dutch, 1 year, No. 2	.50	4.00	
Victoria, 2 year, No. 1	.75	6.00	50.00
Victoria, 2 year, No. 2	.60	5.00	40.00
Victoria, 1 year, No. 1	.60	5.00	40.00
Victoria, 1 year, No. 2	.50	4.00	30.00

BLACKBERRIES

	Per 10	Per 100	Per 1000
Corys Thornless, transpla'ts	$2.00	$15.00	
Corys Thornless, tips	1.50	12.50	$100.00
Evergreen, suckers	.50	3.00	25.00
Evergreen, transplants	.60	5.00	40.00
Himalaya, suckers	.60	4.00	30.00
Himalaya, transplants	.80	6.00	50.00
Lawton, suckers	.50	3.00	25.00
Mammoth, suckers	.70	5.00	40.00
Lucretia Dewberry, transp'ts	.50	3.00	25.00
Lucretia Dewberry, suckers	.60	4.00	35.00

LOGANBERRIES

	Per 10	Per 100	Per 1000
Transplants	$ .75	$ 6.00	$ 50.00
Tips, for spring delivery		3.50	30.00

RASPBERRIES

	Per 10	Per 100	Per 1000
Cumberland, Black, Trans	$ .50	$ 3.50	$ 30.00
Gregg, Black, Transplants	.50	3.50	30.00
Kansas, Black, Transplants	.50	3.50	30.00
Plum Farmer, Black, Transp.	.50	3.50	30.00
Columbia, Purple, Trans	.50	3.50	30.00
Antwerp, Red, Suckers	.40	1.50	12.00
Cuthbert, Red, Suckers	.25	1.50	10.00
King, Red, Suckers	.40	1.50	12.00
Marlboro, Red, Suckers	.40	1.50	12.00
St. Regis, Red, Suckers	.50	3.00	25.00

STRAWBERRIES

From inspected and certified fields
$ .75 per 100, $6.00 per 1000

Ettersburg 121   Gold Dollar   Magoon
Marshall   New Oregon (Banner)

Everbearing varieties, $1.50 per 100, $10.00 per 1000
Progressive   Superb

ASPARAGUS

Palmetto, Connovers Colossal and Argenteuil
1 year—$ .80 per 100; $6.00 per 1000
2 year— 1.00 per 100; 8.00 per 1000

HORSERADISH

$ .30 per 10; $2.00 per 100; $10.00 per 1000

RHUBARB, CROWN DIVISIONS

	Per 10	Per 100	Per 1000
Mammoth Victoria	$ .80	$5.00	$35.00

HORSERADISH

$ .40 per 10, $2.00 per 100, $10.00 per 1000

HOP ROOTS

$ .40 per 10, $3.00 per 100, $20.00 per 1000

SEEDLINGS

COAST GROWN

	Per 1000
Apple, French Crab, No. 1, $\frac{3}{16}$-in. and up	$ 12.00
Apple, French Crab, No. 2, $\frac{1}{8}$ to $\frac{3}{16}$-in	8.00
Pear, French, No. 2, $\frac{1}{8}$ to $\frac{3}{16}$-in	18.00
Pear, French No. 3, about $\frac{1}{8}$-in	15.00
Pear, Japan, No. 1, $\frac{3}{16}$-in. and up	16.00
Pear, Japan, No. 2, $\frac{1}{8}$ to $\frac{3}{16}$-in	12.00
Pear, Japan, No. 3, about $\frac{1}{8}$-in	10.00
Pear, Ussuriensis, No. 1, $\frac{3}{16}$-in. and up	18.00
Pear, Ussuriensis, No. 2, $\frac{1}{8}$ to $\frac{3}{16}$-in	14.00
Pear, Ussuriensis, No. 3, about $\frac{1}{8}$-in	12.00
Cherry, Mazzard, No. 1, $\frac{3}{16}$-in. and up	18.00
Cherry, Mazzard, No. 2, $\frac{1}{8}$ to $\frac{3}{16}$-in	15.00
Cherry, Mazzard, No. 3, about $\frac{1}{8}$-in	12.00
Plum, Myrobolan, No. 1, $\frac{3}{16}$-in. and up	18.00
Plum, Myrobolan, No. 2, $\frac{1}{8}$ to $\frac{3}{16}$-in	16.00
Plum, Myrobolan, No. 3, about $\frac{1}{8}$-in	12.00

A block of Apple Seedlings

NUT TREES

ALMONDS, ONE YEAR

Caliper	Height	Per 10	Per 100	Per 1000
⅝-in. and up	4 -ft. and up....$4.00		$35.00	
½ to ⅝-in.	3½-ft. and up....	3.50	30.00	$250.00
⅜ to ½-in.	3 -ft. and up....	3.00	25.00	200.00
¼ to ⅜-in.	2 -ft. and up....	2.50	20.00	150.00
Drakes	I. X. L.		Ne Plus Ultra	
Nonpariel	Texas			

CHESTNUTS

		Per 10
American Sweet Chestnut ....4-5 ft.		$ 7.50
Spanish Chestnut ....4-5 ft.		7.50

HICKORY

		Per 10
Hickory ....6-8 ft.		$12.50
Hickory ....4-6 ft.		10.00
Hickory ....3-4 ft.		7.50

PECANS

		Per 10
Pecan ....6-8 ft.		$12.50
Pecan ....4-6 ft.		10.00

FILBERTS

	Grade	Per 10	Per 100
Barcelona ....2-3 ft.		$ 5.00	$ 40.00
Barcelona ....1-2 ft.		4.00	30.00
Du Chilly ....2-3 ft.		5.00	40.00
Du Chilly ....1-2 ft.		4.00	30.00

WALNUTS

		Per 10	Per 100	Per 1000
Franquette Grafts	6-8 ft.	$16.50	$150.00	$1350.00
Franquette Grafts	4-6 ft.	13.50	125.00	1150.00
Franquette Grafts	3-4 ft.	12.50	110.00	1000.00
Franquette Seedlings	10-12 ft.	10.00	85.00	
Franquette Seedlings	8-10 ft.	9.50	80.00	
Franquette Seedlings	6-8 ft.	8.50	75.00	

SHADE AND ORNAMENTAL TREES

DECIDUOUS SHADE TREES

	Grade	Per 10	Per 100
Ash, European	6-8 ft.	$5.00	$40.00
Balm of Gilead	8-10	5.00	40.00
Birch, Red or River	8-10	10.00	80.00
Birch, Red or River	6-8	7.50	60.00
Birch, White	12-15	15.00	125.00
Catalpa Speciosa	8-10	6.00	50.00
Catalpa Speciosa	6-8	5.00	40.00
Cherry, Choke	6-8	6.00	50.00
Cherry, Choke	4-6	5.00	40.00
Crab, Bechtels Dbl. Flg.	2-3	5.00	40.00
Dogwood, Native (C. Nuttalli)	6-8	6.00	50.00
Dogwood, Native (C. Nuttalli)	4-6	5.00	40.00
Elm, American White	12-14	8.00	65.00
Elm, American White	10-12	7.50	60.00
Elm, American White	8-10	6.00	50.00
Elm, English	8-10	6.00	50.00
Elm, English	6-8	5.00	40.00
Horse Chestnut	8-10	8.00	70.00
Horse Chestnut	6-8	7.00	60.00
Horse Chestnut	4-6	6.00	50.00
Horse Chestnut	3-4	5.00	40.00
Laburnum (Golden Chain)	6-8	5.00	40.00

DECIDUOUS SHADE TREES--Continued

	Grade	Per 10	Per 100
Locust, Black	10-12	$ 7.50	$50.00
Locust, Black	8-10	4.00	35.00
Locust, Black	6-8	3.00	22.50
Locust, Honey	6-8	5.00	35.00
Locust, Honey	4-6	4.00	30.00
Maple, Norway	10-12	8.00	70.00
Maple, Silver or Soft	8-10	5.00	40.00
Maple, Silver or Soft	6-8	4.00	35.00
Maple, Sugar or Hard	10-12	8.00	70.00
Maple, Sugar or Hard	8-10	7.00	60.00
Maple, Sugar or Hard	6-8	6.00	50.00
Maple, Sycamore	8-10	7.00	60.00
Mulberry, Russian	4-6	3.00	25.00
Poplar, Carolina	10-12	4.00	30.00
Poplar, Carolina	8-10	3.50	25.00
Poplar, Carolina	6-8	2.50	20.00
Poplar, Lombardy	8-10	3.50	25.00
Poplar, Lombardy	6-8	2.50	20.00
Poplar, Silver	8-10	4.00	30.00
Poplar, Silver	6-8	3.50	25.00
Plum, Dbl. Flg (P. Triloba)	4-6	6.00	50.00
Plum, Purple leaf (P Pissardi)	6-8	7.50	60.00
Plum, Purple leaf (P Pissardi)	4-6	6.00	50.00
Thorne, Dbl. Scarlet	4-6	6.00	
Thorne, Dbl. Scarlet	3-4	5.00	

WEEPING TREES

	Grade	Per 10	Per 100
Willow Babylonica	10-12 ft.	$7.00	$60.00
Willow Babylonica	8-10	6.00	50.00
Willow Babylonica	6-8	5.00	40.00

EVERGREEN TREES

	Grade	Per 10	Per 100
Arborvitae, American	3-4 ft.	$8.50	$75.00
Arborvitae, American	2-3	6.00	50.00
Fir, Douglas	4-6	12.50	100.00
Fir, Douglas	2-3	6.00	50.00
Hemlock, Western	2-3	6.00	50.00
Hemlock, Western	18-24 in.	4.00	35.00
Juniper, Irish	3-4 ft.	25.00	
Juniper, Irish	18-24 in.	15.00	
Juniper, Irish	12-18 in.	10.00	
Juniper, Chinese	12-18	12.50	
Juniper, Creeping (Sabina)	18	10.00	
Spruce, Norway	3-4 ft.	15.00	125.00
Spruce, Norway	2-3	12.50	100.00

EVERGREEN SHRUBS

	Grade	Per 10	Per 100
Abelia Grandiflora	12-18 in.	$3.50	
Cotoneaster Floscosa	24-30	8.50	$75.00
Cotoneaster Floscosa	18-24	6.00	50.00
Cotoneaster Floscosa	12-18	3.00	25.00
Cotoneaster Franchetti	24-30	8.50	75.00
Cotoneaster Franchetti	18-24	6.00	50.00
Cotoneaster Franchetti	12-18	3.00	25.00
Cotoneaster Horizontalis	24-30	8.50	75.00
Cotoneaster Horizontalis	18-24	6.00	50.00
Cotoneaster Horizontalis	12-18	3.00	25.00
Cotoneaster Microphylla	24-30	8.50	75.00
Cotoneaster Microphylla	18-24	6.00	50.00
Cotoneaster Microphylla	12-18	3.00	25.00
Cotoneaster Simonsi	24-30	8.50	75.00
Cotoneaster Simonsi	18-24	6.00	50.00
Cotoneaster Simonsi	12-18	3.00	25.00

EVERGREEN SHRUBS—Continued

	Grade	Per 10	Per 100
Cotoneaster Thymifolia	24-30 in.	$8.50	$75.00
Cotoneaster Thymifolia	18-24	6.00	50.00
Cotoneaster Thymifolia	12-18	3.00	25.00
Euonymous, Japonicus	3 in pots	3.00	25.00
Euonymous, Green leaf	18-24 in.	3.50	
Euonymous variegated	12-18	3.50	
Heather, Scotch, 6 varieties	10-12	5.00	
Holly, Budded	4-5 ft.	50.00	
Holly, Budded	3-4	35.00	
Holly, Budded	2-3	25.00	
Holly, English, Seedlings	18-24 in.	15.00	125.00
Laurel, Cherry	12-24	4.50	40.00
Laurel, English	24-30	5.00	
Laurel, English	12-24	4.50	40.00
Laurestinus	12-15	5.00	
Lonicera Nitida	18-24	5.00	
Lonicera Nitida	12-18	4.00	35.00
Lonicera Nitida	10-12	3.00	25.00
Privet, California	2-3 ft.	.50	4.00
Privet, Chinese	3-4	4.00	35.00
Privet, English	1-2	.40	3.50
Veronica Buxifolia	12-18 in.	3.50	
Veronica Buxifolia	8-12	2.50	
Veronica Cupressifolia	12-18	3.50	
Veronica Cupressoides	15-18	5.00	
Veronica Erecta	12-15	2.50	
Veronica Rotundifolia	12-18	3.50	

A charge will be made for balling Evergreen trees and shrubs according to size, as follows:

¾ foot, 25c each   ⅔ foot, 20c each
½ foot, 15s each

HEDGE PLANTS

	Grade	Per 100	Per 1000
Box, Tree	6 in.	$10.00	
Box, Dwarf	4-6	6.00	
Privet, California	2 yr. No. 1	4.00	$35.00
Privet, California	2 yr. No. 2	3.00	25.00
Privet, English or Vulg	1 yr. No. 1	3.50	30.00
Privet, English or Vulg	1 yr. No. 2	2.50	20.00

DECIDUOUS SHRUBS

	Grade	Per 10	Per 100
Berberis Thunbergii	24 in.	$4.00	
Berberis Thunbergii	18-24	3.50	$30.00
Berberis Thunbergii	12-18	2.50	20.00
Buddleia Mag., Butterfly Bush	4-5 ft.	3.50	30.00
Buddleia Mag., Butterfly Bush	4-5	2.50	20.00
Caryopteris (Blue Spirea)	2-3	3.00	
Currant, Red Flowering	2-3	3.50	30.00
Currant, Yellow Flowering	2-3	2.50	20.00
Deutzia Crenata	2-3 ft.	2.50	20.00
Deutzia Crenata	1-2	2.00	15.00
Deutzia Lemoine	2-3	2.50	20.00
Deutzia Lemoine	18-24 in.	2.00	15.00
Deutzia Gracilis	15-18	2.00	15.00
Deutzia Pride of Rochester	4-6 ft.	3.00	25.00
Deutzia Pride of Rochester	3-4	2.50	20.00
Deutzia Pride of Rochester	2-3	2.00	15.00
Deutzia Rosea	4-5	3.00	25.00
Deutzia Rosea	3-4	2.50	20.00
Deutzia Rosea	2-3	2.00	15.00
Deutzia Scabra	3-4	2.50	20.00
Deutzia Scabra Waterii	3-4	3.00	25.00
Elder, Cut leaf	4-6	3.00	25.00
Elder, Red berried	3-4	2.50	20.00
Elder, Silver variegated	4-6	3.00	25.00

DECIDUOUS SHRUBS--Continued

	Grade	Per 10	Per 100
Forsythia Fortunei	3-4 ft.	$3.00	$25.00
Forsythia Fortunei	2-3	2.50	20.00
Forsythia Intermedia	3-4	3.00	25.00
Forsythia Intermedia	2-3	2.50	20.00
Forsythia Suspensa	3	3.00	25.00
Forsythia Suspensa	2-3	2.50	20.00
Genista, Yel. (Scotch Broom)	2-3	2.50	20.00
Genista, white	2-3	3.00	25.00
Genista, Andreana	2-3	3.00	25.00
Genista (Spanish Broom)	2-3	3.50	30.00
Hydrangea, French, pink, white and blue	6 shoots	5.00	
Hydrangea, French, same	4-5 shoots	3.50	
Hydrangea, French, same.	3 shoots	2.50	
Hydrangea Otaksa, Same colors	6 shoots	5.00	
Hydrangea Otaksa, Same colors	4-5 shoots	3.50	25.00
Hydrangea Otaksa, Same colors	3 shoots	2.50	
Kerria Japonica	2-3 ft.	3.50	
Laburnum, (Golden Chain)	2-3	3.50	
Lilac, Common purple	2-3	2.50	20.00
Lilac, Common white	2-3	2.50	20.00
Lonicera Grand, Rosea (Tar. Honeysuckle)	2-3	2.50	20.00
Lonicera Grand, Alba (Tar. Honeysuckle)	2-3	2.50	20.00
Lonicera Morrowi	2-3	2.50	20.00
Olive, Russian	3-4	3.00	25.00
Philadelphus Coronarius	3-4	3.00	25.00
Philadelphus Coronarius	2-3	2.50	20.00
Philadelphus Gordonianus	3-4	3.00	25.00
Philadelphus Lewisi	4-6	6.00	50.00
Philadelphus Nivalis	4-5	3.50	30.00
Philadelphus Zeyheri	3-5	5.00	40.00
Spirea, Anthony Waterer	1-2	2.50	20.00
Spirea Aurea	3-4	3.00	25.00
Spirea Billardi	3-4	3.00	25.00
Spirea Billardi	2-3	2.50	20.00
Spirea Callosa Alba	18-24 in.	2.50	20.00
Spirea Callosa Rubra	18-24	2.50	20.00
Spirea Frobell's	2-3 ft.	2.50	
Spirea Reeve's	18-24 in.	2.50	20.00
Spirea Van Houtte	2-3 ft.	3.00	25.00
Spirea Van Houtte	18-24 in.	2.50	20.00
Spirea Van Houtte	12-18	2.00	15.00
Stephandra Flexuosa	2-3 ft.	5.00	40.00
Sumac (Rhus glabra)	3-4	5.00	40.00
Symphoricarpos Racemosus	2-3	2.50	20.00
Symphoricarpos Vulgaris	2-3	2.50	20.00
Weigela Abel Carriere	2-3	3.00	25.00
Weigela Alba	2-3	3.00	25.00

VINES

	Grade	Per 10	Per 100
Actinidia Polygama	strong	$5.00	$40.00
Ampelopsis Quinquefolia	2 year	1.50	12.50
Ampelopsis Quinquefolia	medium	1.25	10.00
Ampelopsis Veitchii	3 year	3.00	25.00
Ampelopsis Veitchii	2 year	2.50	20.00
Clematis Montana, in pots		3.00	
Clematis Paniculata	large	3.00	
Euonymous Radicans	strong	5.00	40.00
Euonymous Silver variegated	strong	5.00	40.00
Honeysuckle, Belgica	strong	2.00	15.00

	Grade	Per 10	Per 100
Honeysuckle, Fragrantissima	strong	$2.00	$15.00
Honeysuckle, Golden varigtd	strong	2.50	20.00
Honeysuckle Halleana ....strong		2.00	15.00
Ivy, English ....3 year		2.50	20.00
Ivy, English ....4 in. pots		1.00	8.00
Jasmine, White ....2 year		3.00	
Lycium (Matrimony Vine)......strong		2.50	
Wisteria Sinensis, Blue............3 year		3.50	
Wisteria Sinensis, White ....3 year		3.50	

MISCELLANEOUS

	Grade	Per 10	Per 100
Bamboo	6-8 ft.	$3.00	
Lavender (Lavendula vera)......		1.25	
Rosemary		1.25	
Thyme		1.00	$6.00
Vinca, Trailing Myrtle ....2½-in. pots		1.00	6.00
Yucca Filamentosa		5.00	

ROSES

FIELD GROWN, BUDDED

As our Roses are tied in bunches of ten, please make your orders in multiples of that number. When less than five in a variety is ordered, we are obliged to charge the retail price less 25%.

$7.50 per 10; $60.00 per 100

Miss Lolita Armour	Mrs. Chas. E. Shea

$6.00 per 10; $50.00 per 100

Cheerful	Climb. Hoosier Beauty
Cl. Lady Hillingdon	Climb. Sunburst
Cl. Winnie Davis	Colleen
Constance	Edith Part
Golden Emblem	Lady Greenall
Lady Mary Ward	Louise C. Breslau
Marquise de Sinety	May Martin
Mrs. George Gordon	Sunburst

$5.00 per 10; $45.00 per 100

Edward Bohanne	K. of K.
Miss Alice de Rothschild	

$4.50 per 10; $40.00 per 100

Autumn Tints	Billard et Barre
Crimson Emblem	Dorothy Page Roberts
Duchess of Normandy	Duchess of Wellington
Farbenkoenigin	Franz Deegan
Gorgeous	Grange Colomb
Hadley	Harry Kirk
Hoosier Beauty	Irish Elegance
Irish Fireflame	Joseph Hill
Lady Hillingdon	Los Angeles
Lyon	Mdm. Butterfly
Mdm. Edouard Herriott	Mdm. Melanie Soupert
Mdm. Segond Weber	Marechal Neil
Margaret D. Hamill	Miss Kate Moulton
Mrs. Aaron Ward	Mrs. Frank Bray
Old Gold	Pauls Scarlet Climber
Perle von Godesburg	Rayon d'Or
Red Cross	Red Letter Day
Rose Marie	Souv. de Stella Gray

$4.00 per 10; $35.00 per 100

Admiral Ward	Alexander H. Gray
Alfred Colomb	Arthur S. Goodwin
Beauty of Glazenwood	Betty
British Queen	Chateau de C. Vougeot

ROSES--Continued

$4.00 per 10, $35.00 per 100

Cl. Gruss an Teplitz	Cl. Kaiserin A. Victoria
Cl. Maman Cochet White	Columbia
Etoile de Lyon	Geo. C. Waud
Hiawatha	Jonkheer J. L. Mock
Kaiserin A. Victoria	Killarney Queen
Laurent Carle	Mdm. Abel Chatenay
Mdm. Ravary	Mrs. Chas. Russell
Ophelia	Papa Gontier
Persian Yellow	Rhea Reid
T. F. Crozier	White La France
Willowmere	Winnie Davis

$3.50 per 10; $30.00 per 100

Alice Roosevelt	American Beauty
Augustus Hartman	Avoca
Baron de Bonstettin	Baroness Rothschild
Belle Siebrecht	Bessie Brown
Black Prince	Captain Hayward
Cl. Belle Siebrecht	Cl. Frau K. Druschki
Climb. La France	Cl. Mlle. C. Brunner
Cl. Papa Gontier	Climb. Richmond
Clio	Cloth of Gold
Conrad F. Meyer	Dr. O'Donnell Brown
Edward Mawley	Florence Pemberton
Gen. McArthur	George Ahrends
George Dickson	Gloire de C. Guinoisseau
Gloire de Dijon	His Majesty
Hon. Ina Bingham	Hugh Dickson
H. V. Machin	J. B. Clark
Killarney Dbl. White	Killarney Pink
Killarney White	La Detroit
Lady Alice Stanley	Lady Ashtown
Lady Ursula	La France
Mabel Morrison	Mdm. Jules Grolez
Mdm. Leon Simon	Maman Cochet Pink
Maman Cochet White	Marshall P. Wilder
Mary C. of Ilchester	Mlle. Cecile Brunner
Mrs. A. R. Waddell	Mrs. Andrew Carnegie
Mrs. Edward Powell	Mrs. W. C. Miller
Minnie Allen	Moss Crested
Moss Pink	Moss Red
Moss White	National Emblem
Richmond	Soliel d'Or
Wm. A. Richardson	

A corner of two year Rose block. Tree Roses in the foreground.

ROSES—Continued

$3.00 per 10; $25.00 per 100

American Pillar
Dorothy Perkins Pink
General Jacqueminot
Gruss an Teplitz
Mdm. Alfred Carriere
Mrs. John Laing
Paul Neyron
Ragged Robin
Striped Reine Marie H.
Ulrich Brunner

Cl. Mdm. C. Testout
Frau K. Druschki
Gloire Lyonnaise
Juliet
Mdm. Caroline Testout
Mrs. R. G. S. Crawford
Prince C. de Rohan
Reine Marie Henriette
Tausendschoen

BABY RAMBLERS

No. 1 $25.00 per 100;

No. 1A (Extra Heavy) $30.00 per 100

Baby Crimson Rambler
Erna Teschendorf
Mrs. Wm. Cutbush

Baby Tausendschoen
Jessie
Orleans

CLIMBING ROSES AND RAMBLERS
Field Grown, on Own Roots

	Per 10	Per 100	Per 1000
Two year, No. 1	$2.50	$22.50	$200.00
One year, No. 1	2.25	20.00	175.00

American Beauty Cl.
Mdm. Alfred Carriere
Tausendschoen

Flower of Fairfield
Silver Moon

	Per 10	Per 100	Per 1000
Two year, No. 1	$2.00	$17.50	$150.00
One year, No. 1	1.75	15.00	125.00

American Pillar
Blue Rambler
Empress of China
Pink Rambler
Russells Cottage
Yellow Rambler

Baltimore Belle
Dorothy Perkins
Philadelphia Rambler
Queen of Prairie
White Rambler

STANDARD OR TREE ROSES
$1.50 each

Gorgeous
Margaret D. Hamill

Hadley
Mdm. Ed. Herriott

$1.25 each

Constance
Lady Hillingdon

Hoosier Beauty
Los Angeles

75c each

Baby Crimson Rambler
Gruss an Teplitz

Frau Karl Druschki
Mdm. Caroline Testout

HARDY PERENNIALS

$1.25 per dozen; $10.00 per 100 except as otherwise noted.

Alyssum Rostratum, bright golden yellow.
Alyssum Saxatile, bright yellow
Anchusa Italica, Dropmore varieties.
Anemone Japonica, Prince Henry. Rich pink.
Anemone Japonica, Queen Charlotte. Pink.
Anemone Japonica, Whirlwind. Large, white.
Anemone pulsatilla. Purple.
Aquilegia, (Columbine). Choice mixed varieties.
Arabis Alpina fl. pl. Double white.
Armeria Laucheana rosea. Bright rose.
Artichoke, decorative. Gentian blue.
Aster (Michaelmas Daisy) Climax. Lavender, tall.
Aster (Michaelmas Daisy) Amellus. Bluish violet.
Aster (Michaelmas Daisy) Beauty of Colwell. Blue.

18

HARDY PERENNIALS--Continued.

Astilbe Arendsi, Salmon Queen. Salmon pink.
Aubretia Bougainvillei. Deep purple, dwarf.
Bellis perennis (English Daisy). Improved, white, pink.
Bocconia cordata (Plume Poppy). Creamy white.
Campanula medium (Canterbury Bells). Double and single, pink, red, white and purple.
Campanula persicifolia (Peachbells). Double, blue.
Campanula persicifolia Moerheimi. Double white.
Campanula persicifolia. Single, blue or white.
Centaurea (Cornflower or Bachelor Buttons). Blue or white.
Centaurea Dealbata, golden yellow.
Centaurea Montana, violet blue.
Cerastium tormentosum, snow white.
Chelone (Shell Flower) Lyoni. Purplish red.
Chrysanthemum, Hardy Pompon. White, lemon, bronze, crimson and maroon.
Coreopsis lanceolata. Golden yellow.
Delphinium (Larkspur). Mixed.
Dianthus Barbatus (Sweet William). All colors.
Dianthus Deltoides (Maiden Pinks). Pink.
Dianthus plumarius (Garden Pinks). All shades.
Dianthus (Hardy Carnations). Separate shades.
Digitalis (Foxglove). All shades, mixed.
Doronicum Clusii. Early yellow marguerite.
Echinops humilis (Globe Thistle). Deep blue.
Eryngium amethystinum (Sea Holly). Amethyst blue.
Eryngium oliverianum (Sea Holly). Violet.
Gaillardia grandiflora. Red brown.
Geum Heldreichi. Single, orange.
Geum, Mrs. Bradshaw. Double, brilliant scarlet.
Gypsophila paniculata (Baby Breath). Single.
Gypsophila paniculata fl. pl. Double. Raised from seed which usually comes about 25% true, but percentage of double plants can not be guaranteed.
Helenium (Riverton Beauty). Lemon yellow, black center.
Helianthus Newmani. Yellow, dark center.
Heliopsis scabra zinniaflora. Golden yellow.
Hemerocallis (Day Lilly). Yellow.
Hesperis matronalis (Sweet Rocket). White.
Heuchera (Coral Bells) sanguinea. Coral red.
Hibiscus (Marshmallow) Moscheutos. Rose red.
Hollyhocks. Double. All colors.
Hypericum Moserianum (St. Johnswort). Yellow.
Iberis sempervirens (Hardy Candytuft). White.
Inula glandulosa. Orange yellow.
Iris, German. Varieties:
  Atropurpurea. Dwarf. Rich purple.
  Caprice. Rosy red.
  Caterina. Blue, falls shaded lilac.
  Crimson King. Claret and purple.
  Flavescens. Large, fragrant, yellow.
  Florentina alba. Dwarf, pure white.
  Gypsy Queen. Old gold, falls yellow.
  Juniata. Clear blue.
  Lohengrin. Rosy mauve.
  Mdm. Chereau. Tall, blue edged white.
  Nibelungen. Fawn yellow.
  Pallida dalmatica. Fragrant, light lavender.
  Prince Victor. Blue, falls lavender.
  Princess Victoria Louise. Sulphur yellow.
  Queen of May. Soft rose.
Iris, Japanese. Mixed shades.
Jerusalem Cross.
Linum perenne (Perennial Flax). Blue.
Lobelia cardinalis. Rich fiery red.

Lupinus (Lupine). Blue, white, pink.
Myosotis palustris (Forget-me-not). Blue.
Paeonia (Peony), 35c each, $3.00 per 10.
    Festiva Maxima. Large, white.
    Golden Harvest. Center light yellow, edged pink.
    Queen Victoria. White, center creamy.
Papaver nudicaule (Iceland Poppy). All shades.
Papaver orientale (Oriental Poppy). Fiery red.
Papaver orientale, Perry's White. Satiny white.
Papaver orientale, Salmon Queen. Salmon pink.
Penstemon gloxinioides. Bright shades.
Phlox, Hardy:
    Le Mahdi. Deep purple.
    Miss Lingard. Tall, pure white.
    Mrs. Jenkins. Dwarf, pure white.
Phlox subulata lilacina. Light lilac.
Phlox subulata rosea. Light rose.
Physostegia virginica (False Dragonhead). Soft pink.
Physostegia virginica alba. White.
Potentilla atrosanguinea. Rich crimson.
Primroses. Mixed shades.
Pyrethrum (Persian Daisy). Double, rose, red, white.
Pyrethrum (Persian Daisy). Single, pink, white, bluish pink.
Rudbeckia (Golden Glow). Golden yellow.
Salvia azurea (Meadow Sage). Sky blue.
Saxifraga Megasea crassifolia. Rosy pink.
Shasta Daisy.
Solidago (Golden Rod). Golden yellow.
Statice (Great Sea Lavender) latifolia.
Stokesia Cyanea (Cornflower Aster). Lavender blue.
Thalictrum (Meadow Rue) aquilegifolium. Rosy pink.
Thalictrum glacum. Bronze yellow.
Tritoma Pfitzeri (Red-hot Poker). Rich orange scarlet.
Valariana coccinea (Valerian). Deep red.
Viola (Tufted Pansies) Blue Perfection. Purplish blue.
Viola (Tufted Pansies) lutea splendens. Rich golden yellow.
Violets, Princess of Wates.
Veronica (Speedwell) spicata alba. White.
Veronica (Speedwell) spicata atropurpurea. Purple.
Wallflowers, Aloui. Golden yellow.
Wallflowers, Goliath. Brownish red.
Wallflowers. Mixed varieties.

NURSERYMEN'S SUPPLIES

BEST VALUES AT MINIMUM PRICES

NURSERY KNIVES: Hand forged, and thoroughly tested; bought direct from the factory, thus saving the jobber's profit.

Knives ordered at the single rate will be forwarded by mail prepaid.

HOLLY MANUFACTURING CO.'S—Always satisfactory.

Paring Knife, 50c each; $5.00 per dozen.

Pocket Grafter No. 11023, 75c each; $7.50 per dozen.

Pocket Budder, brass lined, No. 15095, $1.25 each; $12.50 per dozen.

No. 15096, exactly like No. 15095 except that it has a bone tip for opening the bark, $1.50 each. $15.00 per dozen.

Stationary Handle Budder, 50c each; $5.00 per dozen

22

Pocket Pruner No. 11092. $1.50 each; $15.00 per dozen.

Stationary Handle Grafter No. 1, 60c each; $6.00 per dozen.
Stationary Handle Grafter No. 2, same as No. 1 but lighter. 60c each; $6.00 per dozen.

23

Pocket Pruner No. 11089, with countersunk hole for Key Ring, $1.40 each; $14.00 per dozen.

Pocket Pruner No. 14089. Same as No. 11089 except Stag Handle. $1.40 each; $14.00 per dozen.

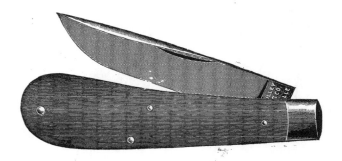

Pocket Budder, Steel Lined, No. 11097. 75c each; $7.50 per dozen.

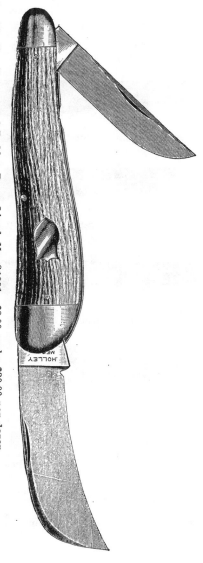

Combination Pruner and Budder, Brass Lined, No. 21991. $2.00 each; $20.00 per dozen.
Combination Grafter and Budder, Brass Lined, No. 21990. $2.00 each; $20.00 per dozen.

HARRINGTON CUTLERY CO'S Dexter Shoe Knife. Many of our customers have used these a good many years for Scion Knives and will have no other. Either 2-in. or 2½-in. blade, 30c each; $3.00 per dozen.

J. A. HENKELS TWIN WORKS CUTLERY

Pocket Budder No. 715B. $1.50 each; $15.00 per dozen.

Pocket Budder No. 717B, Bone tip that closes. $1.75 each; $20.00 per dozen.

Stationary Handle Pruner No. 305½, 90c each; $9.00 per dozen.

Stationary Handle Grafter No. 304½, 75c each; $7.50 per dozen.

Stationary Handle Grafter No. 303½, 60c each; $6.00 per dozen.

Stationary Handle Budder No. 302½, 50c each; $5.00 per dozen.

Stationary Handle Paring Knife No. 306½. Same size as Budder. 50c each; $5.00 per dozen.

Pruning Shears, No. 205 8½ inch, double brass springs, $2.50 each; $27.50 per dozen.

Pruning Shears, No. 190, 7½-in. volute spring, $2.25 each; $22.50 per dozen.

Pruning Shears, No. 23, 6½-in. full polished, $2.00 each; $20.00 per dozen.

Pruning Shears, No. 23, 5½-in. full polished, $1.75 each; $17.50 per dozen.

PRUNING SHEARS, Pexto Brand

No. R85—8½-in. Full polished, double brass springs, $2.00 each, $20.00 per dozen.

No. R65—9-in. Full polished, double brass springs, $1.75 each, $17.50 per dozen.

No. 14—6-in. Full polished, nickel plated, volute springs, $1.25 each, $12.50 per dozen

No. R70—9-in. Straw colored blades, volute springs, $1.75 each, $17.50 per dozen.

No. R50—9-in. Straw colored blades, volute springs, $1.25 each, $12.50 per dozen.

No. 50—8-in. Straw colored blades, volute springs, $1.00 each, $10.00 per dozen.

PAPER

Mosinee Kraft.

A strong tough paper that withstands moisture well, therefore ideal for nursery use.

36-in., about 50 lbs. to the roll, 12c per lb.

Keepdry. Muslin lined, waterproof, 36-in., 100 yds. to roll, $7.00 per roll.

Same construction, heavier paper, $7.50 per roll.

Keepdry, reinforced with diagonal crossed **yarns**, waterproof. same size rolls, $6.00 per roll.

Same construction, heavier paper $6.50 per roll.

Grizzly Bear Ripplecraft. Waterproof, elastic. 36 inch. 100 yard rolls, 16c per pound.

Burlap. 8 ounce, 40 inch, bolt lots, about 100 **yards**, 8½c per yard.

Three dial machines, can be turned back to zero on completing the count of each variety....................$12.00
These can also be furnished with four dials at.. 16.00
Or five dials at 20.00

LABELS

We keep on hand a supply of the Benj. Chase Co.'s 3½-inch Plain and Painted Tree Labels, and Plain and Painted Pot Labels which can be shipped on short notice in sizes and at the prices named below:

1000 in package, except where otherwise listed.

		Per 1000
Plain Iron wired Tree Labels..............3½x ⅝-in.		$1.60
Painted Iron wired Tree Labels........3½x ⅝-in.		2.00
Plain Copper wired Tree Labels...... 3½x ⅝-in.		1.90
Painted Copper wired Tree Labels.. 3½x ⅝-in.		2.30
Plain Pot Labels .... 4 x ⅝-in.		1.30
Painted Pot Labels .... 4 x ⅝-in.		1.70
Plain Pot Labels .... 5 x ⅝-in.		1.60
Painted Pot Labels .... 5 x ⅝-in.		2.10
Plain Pot Labels .... 6 x ⅝-in.		2.00
Painted Pot Labels................ 6 x ⅝-in.		2.50
Painted Pot Labels, 250 in ctn..........10 x ⅝-in.		5.80
Painted Pot Labels 250 in ctn..........12 x ⅝-in.		7.00
Painted Garden Labels, 250 in ctn .. 8 x ⅞-in.		6.50
Painted Garden Labels, 100 in ctn..12 x1⅛-in.		11.00

We will fill orders for Printed or Plain Labels to be shipped direct from the factory, at the manufacturers' price, giving you the regular factory discount, which is as follows:

Less than 6,000...List price
6,000 to 40,000..10% discount
40,000 to 80,000..15% discount
80,000 to 130,000..20% discount
130,000 and over..25% discount

1, 2 and 3 ply White Sisal on spools of about **70** lbs., or put up in 5 lb. balls, 10 balls to sack, **18c** per lb.

Maylasia Fine, 2 and 3 ply, more than double footage to the lb. than you get in Sisal, 23c per **lb.**

2 and 3 ply Clover-leaf Manila, medium, 5 **lb.** balls., per lb. 23c.

2 and 3 ply Clover-leaf Manila, fine, 5 lb. balls, 25c per lb.

Standard Binding Twine, 5 lb. balls, 15c per lb.
2 ply packing Twine, made of 2 strands Binding Twine, 5 lb. balls, 15c per lb.
The higher priced Twines are the most economical to use, as they run a much greater number of feet to the pound.

ORCHARD YARN

1-ply, tarred, 5-lb. Balls.............................15c per **lb.**
2-ply, tarred, 5-lb. Balls.............................15c per **lb.**

RAFFIA

Westcoast Brand.   Small lots, 20c per lb.

Twine. Extra quality Cotton Budding Twine, **3 or** 4 ply, 5 lb. sacks, 60c per lb.

TREE GAUGES

Circular, convenient to carry in pocket. Measures both fractions of an inch and millimeters, 60c each; $6.00 per dozen.

SHINGLE TOW

Cedar Shingle tow, put up in bales. Car lots, R. R. Co's weight, $9.00 per ton, less than car lots, $11.00 per ton, F. O. B.

The mill is working on our orders now and if order is placed soon it will insure shipment in time for fall packing.

HORSE MUZZLES

60c each, $6.00 per dozen.

AMES TAPER NURSERY SPADES

D handle, strapped full length, $3.00 each, $32.50 per dozen.

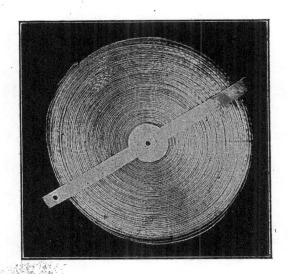

STRAP IRON

⅝ inch, on reels, containing 300 feet. $2.00 per reel.

Strap Iron, ⅝ inch, cut to 12 inch lengths. Put up in boxes of 100 lbs. each. $10.00 per box. Smaller quantities, 11c per pound.

One of our blocks of Myrobolan Seedlings on
the Columbia Highway east of the city.

CPSIA information can be obtained
at www.ICGtesting.com
Printed in the USA
BVHW041055271218
536518BV00006B/131/P

9 780265 928899